⬧ BIG LEAGUE
SPRING TRAINING

•••• GEORGE SULLIVAN

BIG
LEAGUE
SPRING
TRAINING

◆ HENRY HOLT AND COMPANY ◆ NEW YORK ◆

Library of Congress Cataloging-in-Publication Data
Sullivan, George.
  Big league spring training / by George Sullivan. — 1st
ed.
      p. cm.
  Summary: Describes a big league baseball spring-
training camp.
  Bibliography: p.
  Includes index.
  ISBN 0-8050-0838-1
  1. Baseball—Training. I. Title.
GV875.6.S85   1989
796.357′64′0973—dc19   88-28423

Copy 1 2/90 Follett 13.46

First Edition
Designer: Victoria Hartman
Printed in the United States of America
10 9 8 7 6 5 4 3 2 1

✦ ACKNOWLEDGMENTS

Many people helped me in preparing this book, in particular the officials of several major league baseball clubs. Special thanks are due Larry Shenk, vice president, public relations, of the Philadelphia Phillies, who called my home in response to a letter from me and said to my wife in my absence, "Tell George the Phillies are ready to welcome him when he arrives in Clearwater." That started the ball rolling. Special thanks are also due Howard Starkman, Toronto Blue Jays; Dan Ewald, Detroit Tigers; Harvey Greene, Lou D'Ermilio, and Ann Melio, New York Yankees; Patricia Kelly, National Baseball Hall of Fame; Don Miers, Osceola County Stadium and Sports Complex; Jay Alves, Oakland Athletics; Larry Babcock, California Angels; Dan Pearson, Boardwalk and Baseball; Valerie Arcuri, Cleveland Indians; Terry Reynolds, Dodgertown; Craig Sanders, Houston Astros; Francesca Kurti, TLC Custom Labs; and, for service far beyond the call of duty, Carole and Jack Moran.

G.S.

◆ CONTENTS

◆ BIG LEAGUE
SPRING TRAINING

1 ◇ Spring Ritual

Early one morning during the second week in February, a tractor trailer rolls up to Yankee Stadium in New York's borough of the Bronx. Into it will be loaded twenty-four trunks of baseball gear; two hundred uniforms; two hundred bats; stacks of medical supplies, weights, and odd-looking weight-training equipment; three exercise bikes; two pitching machines; dozens of boxes of Yankee jackets, plastic helmets, and other souvenirs to be sold at concession stands; and a silvery cart with a big yellow-and-blue umbrella from which hot dogs will be sold.

It takes ten men all day to load the truck. By nightfall it is heading south. A few days later it arrives in Fort Lauderdale, Florida, site of the Yankees' spring-training camp.

Outside Yankee Stadium, a tractor trailer is loaded with baseball gear. The truck's destination: the Yankees' spring-training camp at Ft. Lauderdale, Florida. (George Sullivan)

At about the same time, that scene is being duplicated outside the ballparks of the other twenty-five major league baseball teams. The cargo loaded into the trucks is similar, but the destination for each is different. Eight clubs train in southern Arizona; the eighteen other sites are scattered throughout Florida.

When those big trucks begin arriving at their destinations, it signals the beginning of baseball's annual ritual of spring training. The snow in most of the northern half of the country may be four feet deep and news of basketball and hockey may be filling the sports pages, but suddenly it's time for baseball again.

There are two reasons for spring training: to get players ready for the season and to inspect and evaluate players who may be ready to play in the major leagues.

Spring training lasts six to seven weeks. Pitchers and catchers report in mid-February, two to three weeks ahead of the rest of the squad. This gives the pitchers time to loosen up their arms before having to face the hitters.

At the end of February or in very early March, the other members of the team join the pitchers and catchers. Daily workouts begin.

All teams go to spring training to pitch and hit—that is, to get pitchers' arms ready and give hitters all the batting practice they want. Some teams pitch and hit and do little else. Other teams put an emphasis on drills that are meant to school players in baseball's basic skills—fielding, throwing, running, sliding, and bunting.

More and more, in fact, managers are using their coaching staffs to teach fundamentals during spring training. Because players nowadays generally spend only a couple

Slugger Kirk Gibson tries his hand at bunting at the Dodgers'
training camp, Vero Beach, Florida.
(© Los Angeles Dodgers, 1988)

of years in the minor leagues, which is much less time than
they used to spend, instruction on a major league level
has taken on greater importance.

When the Philadelphia Phillies opened spring-training
camp in 1988, Manager Lee Elia announced a strong emphasis on teaching. The forty-five days the team was to
spend in Clearwater, Florida, was to be divided into three
parts. "The first fourteen days are mainly for conditioning
and touching upon the fundamentals," said Elia. "The
next seventeen days are for judging young players and

Toronto's Cecil Fielder (23) pursues Glenallen Hill (30) during base-running drill. Third player is Manny Lee. (George Sullivan)

nonroster invitees, while also going strong on fundamentals. And the last fourteen days are for reviewing those fundamentals, setting up all our plays for the regular season, making the final cuts, and gearing up for the season."

Visit a camp late in February or during the early weeks of March and you'll see pitchers practicing covering first base, outfielders throwing to the cutoff man, and infielders working on rundown plays and different formations for defending against bunts.

Intrasquad games begin around March 1. Exhibition games start soon after. Unlike the regular season, wherein clubs never play outside their leagues, springtime competition often pits American League clubs against those representing the National League.

Teams that train in Florida compete in what is known as the Grapefruit League. In Arizona it's the Cactus

League. Wins and losses are recorded in a combined standings for both of the leagues. No one pays very much attention to them, however. And on the opening day of the regular season, they're forgotten.

For the players spring training can be pleasant. "After the winter it's good to be back with the guys," said Steve Lake, a catcher with the St. Louis Cardinals, once spring training opened in 1988. "When you've had a good season [the Cards won the National League championship in 1987], you can't wait to put the uniform back on."

Pro football training camps, which open in mid-July, are very different from baseball camps. Football players must attend classes to learn plays and strategy. There are thick playbooks that must be memorized and sweat-soaked scrimmages with plenty of hard hitting.

Pro football players live in college dormitories. Everything runs according to a strict schedule that goes from sunup to sundown. There are no friends or families around.

Baseball, by contrast, is a picnic. The sky is blue. The sun is warm. Palm trees sway in the gentle breezes.

"For a ballplayer spring in Florida can be a great family time," says Bob Forsch, a veteran pitcher for the Cardinals.

Forsch and his wife have two girls, ages nine and twelve. During the regular season Bob doesn't get a chance to spend very much time with them. "They're asleep every night when I get home from the ballpark," he says. "In order to spend time with them, I get up and drive the girls to school."

But during spring training it's different. "My family can't wait to get to Florida," Forsch says. "We rent a house there. My work day ends early. My wife and the girls can go to the beach, or maybe Busch Gardens. I can even get in a little fishing."

What can the fans expect to see at spring training?

They can expect to see their favorite players up close. Baseball in the spring is much more relaxed than during the regular season, especially during the last weeks of February and early weeks of March. Many players enjoy talking with the fans, chatting about the season ahead or the ups and downs of the season just past. Players are often willing to sign autographs and pose for photographs.

Fans can enjoy the games more because they're so close to the action. Parks in Florida and Arizona are built to accommodate five or six thousand fans, not fifty or sixty thousand. Watching a game in spring training is something like watching a game at a high school field. Not only do you see everything well, but you overhear the joking comments of players during batting practice; you hear the infielders as they shout encouragement to the pitcher.

"After seeing baseball in Florida, I'd rather watch the game on TV than go to a major league stadium," says one fan. "The small park spoils you. You sit so close, you can almost reach out and touch the players. You don't get that feeling at a big league stadium."

Late in February and during the first week in March, before games are scheduled, teams hold workouts every day. The entire squad is involved. Fans see many different kinds of fielding and base-running drills. In fact, there are so many things going on at once, it may look helter-skelter, but it's all highly organized. It's fun to watch, particularly if you know the team well enough to be able to

Camera-carrying fans of the Toronto Blue Jays arrive at the team's Dunedin, Florida, headquarters to watch a practice session. (George Sullivan)

identify the players. It's like watching a rehearsal.

At many of the major league training sites, there's a good chance of coming face to face with a Hall of Famer, even a baseball legend. Whitey Ford and Mickey Mantle are often in residence at the Yankees' camp in Fort Lauderdale. Their former teammate Yogi Berra is now a coach for the Houston Astros, who train in Kissimmee.

Al Kaline can be found among the Tigers in Lakeland. Ted Williams serves as a springtime batting coach for the Boston Red Sox, who headquarter in Winter Haven. In Vero Beach fans can run into Sandy Koufax of Dodger fame.

Of course, fans can also expect to see players they've

Hall of Famer Yogi Berra, once a Yankee star, is now a coach for the Houston Astros. (Osceola County Stadium & Sports Complex; Loretta Lombardy)

never heard of before and perhaps will never hear of again. Spring training is a time of testing and evaluating. The manager and the coaches want to look at new players. This means that there are a great many rookies and some minor leaguers, particularly during the first weeks of the season.

Spring training is a time for answering questions: How will the rookie newcomers do? Will they live up to expectations?

How about the veteran players attempting comebacks? Veteran pitchers will be testing injured arms; hitters will be trying to show they can still hit.

Other players are being tried at new positions. Will these experiments succeed?

Still others, traded during the off-season, are playing with new teams. How will the new surroundings affect them? How will their old teams get along without them?

The Phillies face the St. Louis Cardinals in preseason game at Jack Russell Stadium, Clearwater, Florida. (George Sullivan)

Spring training is a time of great expectations. Managers talk about how well their veteran players are rounding into shape and express nothing but optimism about the rookies.

All teams are undefeated. All are tied for first place. On opening day of the season, the first Monday in April, reality will take over. But in spring training everyone is filled with hope and confidence.

② Looking Back

Major league baseball teams have been training in the South for well over a century. The very first efforts to play in warmer, southern climates took place in the late 1860s. William "Boss" Tweed, a powerful political figure of the day, sent his New York Mutuals to New Orleans in 1869 to play local teams. The Cincinnati Red Stockings, who had won 56 games in 1869, and the Chicago White Stockings journeyed to New Orleans late in the winter of 1870 for exhibition games.

However, most baseball historians cite 1886 as the year the first spring-training camp was formally established. That was the year that Adrian "Cap" Anson took the Chicago White Stockings to Hot Springs, Arkansas. Anson ordered daily twenty-mile hikes to get his players into shape.

Two years later a National League team representing Washington, D.C., boarded a train to Jacksonville, Florida, for spring workouts. Baseball was a scruffy, ragtag business in those days, and the Washington players were refused rooms in one hotel after another. When the players

Billy Werber slides home as Rick Ferrell gets set to make the tag at the Boston Red Sox training camp at Sarasota, Florida, in 1932. (United Press International)

were finally accepted, it was only on the condition that they not mingle with the other guests or eat in the hotel dining room.

Although managers and owners were beginning to see the advantage of going south to get their teams into shape before the season opened, it wasn't until 1908 that the first permanent spring-training camp was established. Marlin Springs, Texas, was the site. John McGraw brought the New York Giants there. The team had ended up second to the Chicago Cubs the season before. Although the Giants finished as runners-up to the Cubs again in 1909, they had demonstrated that Texas was attractive for spring

Modern Al Lang Stadium in St. Petersburg, home grounds for the St. Louis Cardinals each spring, is named in honor of the "father of Florida baseball." (George Sullivan)

training. Within a few years several other teams were working out there.

After World War I ended in 1918, interest began to shift to Florida, largely through the efforts of Al Lang, who is now known as the father of Florida baseball. Lang had moved from Pittsburgh to St. Petersburg in 1911. There he became a successful businessman and later the town's mayor.

In 1914, three years after Lang arrived in Florida, Branch Rickey took the St. Louis Browns to St. Petersburg for spring training. Lang was quick to see the economic benefits of having a baseball team on hand for a couple of months. The team attracted tourists. The tourists spent money.

In 1922, thanks to Lang's effort, Waterfront Park opened in St. Petersburg. The Boston Braves, who had been training in Galveston, Texas, moved there and stayed through 1937. Lang was also successful in luring the Brooklyn Dodgers to Clearwater, about ten miles north of St. Petersburg, in 1923. And he got the New York Giants to set up shop in Sarasota, some twenty miles south of St. Petersburg, also in 1923.

Lang's biggest coup was landing the New York Yankees, the most popular team of the day. The Yanks gave up New Orleans for Crescent Lake Park in St. Petersburg in 1925.

By 1929 ten of the sixteen major league teams were holding their spring training in Florida.

Although Florida continued to grow in popularity, some teams turned to foreign sites for spring training. As early as 1913 the Yankees traveled to Hamilton, Bermuda. While there, Hal Chase, the team's star first baseman, fell off a bicycle and broke a leg. The Yankees never returned to Bermuda.

Cuba has been tried too. The New York Giants traveled to Havana in 1937. The Brooklyn Dodgers held their spring training in Havana for three consecutive years in the early 1940s. The Giants eventually settled upon Arizona, while the Dodgers switched from Cuba to Florida.

Al Lang, for his efforts on behalf of the Sunshine State, has not been forgotten. Al Lang Stadium, built in 1977 and now the springtime home of the St. Louis Cardinals, was named in his honor.

Anyone who wants to experience what spring training was like in the distant past has only to visit McKechnie

The Brooklyn Dodgers tried Havana, Cuba, for spring training during the early 1940s. This was a scene in 1942.
(Wide World Photos)

Field in Bradenton, Florida, presently home grounds of the Pittsburgh Pirates. McKechnie Field dates to 1923, and since that time seven major league teams besides the Pirates have used McKechnie Field. It is named after former Pirate Manager Bill McKechnie. A Hall of Famer, McKechnie died in 1962.

When you visit McKechnie Field, it's like stepping into baseball's past. The 5,000 seats are not plastic or concrete; you sit on wooden benches. Tin covers the grandstand roof and outfield fences. When a foul ball strikes the roof, it sounds like a metal garbage can being dropped onto concrete from a twelfth-story window.

In 1988 Cardinal players
wore this arm patch
to salute fifty years
of spring training
in St. Petersburg.
(George Sullivan)

The old Bradenton ballpark was home first to the St. Louis Cardinals. Over the years many of baseball's all-time greats have performed there. Dizzy Dean, the wacky St. Louis Cardinal, pitched at McKechnie Field. Dean also owned a gas station in town. Babe Ruth played there. The Yankees used to take a ferryboat across the mouth of Tampa Bay from their spring-training grounds in St. Petersburg for games in Bradenton.

Hank Aaron, who was to break Babe Ruth's all-time home run record, spent his first Florida spring training at McKechnie Field. Aaron was playing for the Milwaukee Braves at the time.

"This park has a little rust and a little age," John Wiand, a 47-year-old resident of St. Petersburg, told the *St. Petersburg Times*. "It reminds you of yesteryear."

Of course, some changes have been made through the years. The clubhouse down the left-field line has been

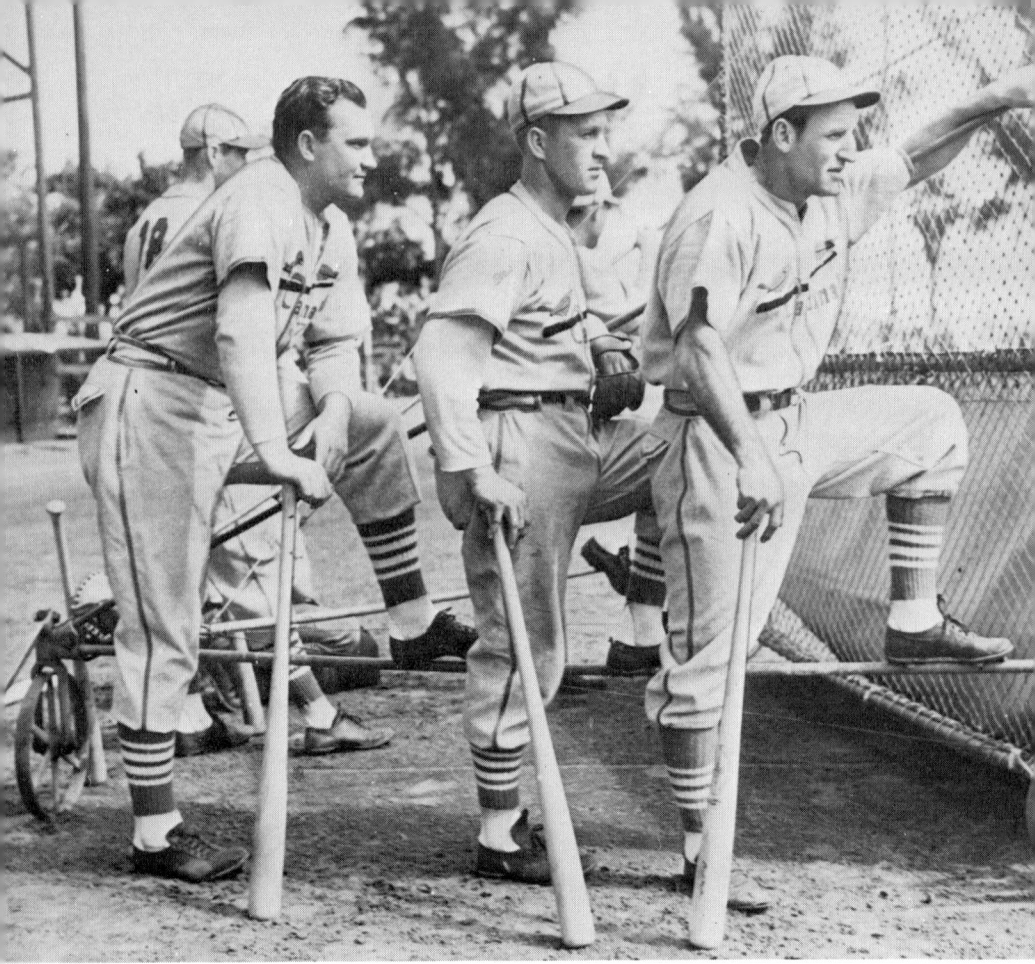

Cardinal sluggers (left to right) Johnny Mize, Enos Slaughter, and Pepper Martin pose at the batting cage. Scene is in St. Petersburg, Florida, in 1929.
(United Press International)

fenced in. (But it's still easy to catch players going to and from it before and after games.) Batting cages have been added down the right-field line. The restrooms and concession stands have been fixed up. And after Whitey Herzog, manager of the St. Louis Cardinals, complained that the outfield was the closest thing to a cow pasture he had ever seen, new outfield grass was put down.

"But we haven't changed the important thing," Ken

Carlson, the 73-year-old secretary of the Bradenton Boosters, told the *St. Petersburg Times.* "We haven't changed the place's charm."

Nowadays most teams remain at the training camps until a few days before the regular season, and then they are whisked home. But in the days before big jets, when teams traveled by train, they often played their way back home. In so doing, the club could recover training-camp expenses and perhaps even earn a profit.

One team would pair with another. The two would travel on the same train, stopping in a different town each day to play.

Players bunked in small compartments called roomettes. As the train approached the town where they were to play, players would change into their uniforms. After the game they'd return to the train in their uniforms, there to shower and change.

The Cleveland Indians and New York Giants had a long series of spring rivalries. Both clubs trained in Arizona. In mid-March they would break camp and head east, traveling in a special five-car train. There were two cars for each team—one for the players, the other for club officials and the press. The fifth car was a dining car.

The train would make stopovers in such cities and towns as Wichita Falls and Paris, Texas; Shreveport, Louisiana; and Louisville, Kentucky.

Third baseman Al Rosen, a star player with the Indians and the American League's Most Valuable Player in 1953, remembers those days fondly. "You could learn a lot of baseball from talking with the older players on those trips,"

Rosen once told *The Sporting News*. "We'd all congregate in the washroom at the end of the Pullman car. There'd be a big, padded seat where three or four fellows would sit, and the rest would stand. We'd have maybe a drink or two and talk baseball right into the night.

"You'd talk to those good hitters the Giants had, like Walker Cooper, Monte Irvin, Al Dark, and Bobby Thomson, and you'd pick up a lot. I know I did."

During World War II, when travel restrictions were in force because of a fuel shortage, clubs had to revise their spring-training plans. Kenesaw Mountain Landis, the commissioner of baseball, ordered teams to hold their spring workouts close to home.

This was a time before expansion, when all the major league teams were located on or east of the Mississippi River. None of the clubs had invaded the Southern states. There were no teams in California, Texas, or Georgia. Instead of romping around on sun-splashed diamonds, players had to train indoors—in college field houses, National Guard armories, and even school gymnasiums.

The Boston Red Sox, for example, trained at Tufts University in Medford, Massachusetts. The Braves, who were also based in Boston at the time, journeyed to the Choate School in Wallingford, Connecticut. The New York Yankees trained at Asbury Park, New Jersey, in 1943, then moved farther south to Atlantic City for 1944 and 1945.

The Brooklyn Dodgers went north, to a state park in Bear Mountain, New York, not far from West Point. One year while they were there a March blizzard forced the team to cancel outdoor workouts. Photographers got players to pose throwing snowballs as well as baseballs.

First workout for the New York Giants at their Lakewood, New Jersey, training camp in 1944. (United Press International)

After the war ended, most teams went back to Florida. There were a couple that didn't, however. The Cleveland Indians, in 1947, established training headquarters in Tucson, Arizona. The New York Giants also selected Arizona that year. The Giants picked Phoenix.

The Chicago Cubs moved to Mesa, Arizona, in 1952. Before that, the Cubs had trained at Catalina Island, just off the coast of Southern California, a site convenient to Pasadena, California, home of the team's owner, Philip Wrigley.

In the spring of 1937 radio station WHO in Des Moines,

Iowa, sent a sports announcer to Catalina Island to cover the Cubs. While in California the announcer took time out for a screen test, which proved successful. Soon after, the announcer quit his radio job and became a Hollywood actor, turning out one film after another during the 1940s. He went from a film and later a television career to a job as president of the United States. His name, of course, was Ronald Reagan.

The newer West Coast teams—the Seattle Mariners, California Angels, San Diego Padres, and Oakland Athletics—all enjoy the convenience of Arizona for spring training.

The Milwaukee Brewers do too. Why do the Brewers trek all the way from Milwaukee to Chandler, Arizona, each February? Florida is several hundred miles closer. It has to do with the team's heritage. The Brewers were founded as the Seattle Pilots in 1969. As a West Coast team, the Pilots trained in Arizona. The following year, when the American League expanded from ten to twelve teams, the Seattle franchise was switched to Milwaukee. But the club saw no reason to give up its spring base in Chandler.

Players, coaches, managers, and owners debate whether it's Florida or Arizona that offers the best conditions for spring training. If the choice were left to the players, most would probably pick Florida.

Those players who are familiar with both sites complain that the Arizona air is so dry that it is difficult to work up a good sweat. And many players identify sweating with loosening up and shedding extra pounds.

The truth is that one sweats just as much in the low-humidity heat of Arizona as in Florida, where the humidity is likely to be high. But in low-humidity heat, moisture evaporates faster. It *seems* to the players that they don't sweat as much.

Another complaint also has to do with the thinness of the air in Arizona, the complete lack of humidity. The ball travels higher and farther in dry air. Home runs can occur with amazing frequency. Sure, players like to hit home runs, but most prefer playing under the more realistic conditions that Florida offers.

Pitchers complain the loudest. All those home runs are depressing.

A third difference between Arizona and Florida has to do with the sky, or at least how the sky appears. In Arizona the sky is usually cloudless and very blue. Players say it's a "high" sky. "It looks a million miles high," says one. However it's described, the Arizona sky can be troublesome for outfielders. They say pop flies are harder to catch. Even the best have problems occasionally.

There's one other difference, and it has to do with the facilities for training. In Florida an era of great change is underway. Ramshackle ballparks with bleacher seats and wooden fences, as typified by McKechnie Field, are fast going the way of baggy uniforms and Sunday double-headers. They're being replaced by modern stadiums and multifield practice layouts, carpeted clubhouses and meeting rooms, and recreational and medical facilities. In Florida spring training is being transformed.

3 ◆ A New Era

Wwhat every team wants today is one giant complex where the players on the major league roster and the entire minor league system can train together. That means having major and minor league clubhouses, a cluster of practice diamonds that a manager can view from an observation tower, and a modern stadium that can seat seven to eight thousand spectators.

Complexes of this type are baseball factories. They're always busy. Not only do they have complete facilities for all spring-training activities, they're also used during the summer for competition by teams in the Florida State League, a minor league, and, in some cases, for games between local high schools and colleges. And during the

Boardwalk and Baseball, near Haines City, Florida, with its modern stadium, cluster of practice fields, and other facilities, is the last word in training complexes. It's spring headquarters for the Kansas City Royals.
(Boardwalk and Baseball; Tom Hurst)

winter months, they're busy with the Instructional League, a league that provides schooling for young and promising minor leaguers.

The Dodgers were the first team to train at such a site. In the years following World War II, the Dodgers, who represented Brooklyn at the time (the club moved to Los Angeles after the 1957 season), were approached by Bud Holman, a businessman from the town of Vero Beach. The federal government had just handed over to the town a training center for World War II bomber pilots. The base covered 109 acres and boasted two huge, barrackslike structures that could accommodate as many as a thousand ballplayers. Holman wanted to know whether the Dodgers would be interested in the facility as a training site. Indeed the Dodgers were. The club began training at Vero Beach in 1945. Even after the club shifted operations to the West Coast, the Dodgers continued to train at Vero Beach, first renting the site, later purchasing it.

Vero Beach triggered a new day in spring training. Because of its enormous size, it was possible to have players from every level, from the major league team down to the lowliest minor leaguers, together in one camp. Once the Dodger camp was in operation, every other team in baseball sought to imitate what the Dodgers had done.

Now called Dodgertown, the Dodger training camp has gone through many changes since the team first began using it. The old barracks have been replaced by a modern, ninety-unit apartment house. A sprawling administration building was completed in 1974. That's where the clubhouses are located. The building also houses a dining room and kitchen, medical facilities, a trainer's room, an inter-

Holman Stadium, centerpiece of the Dodgertown complex at
Vero Beach, Florida. (Los Angeles Dodgers)

view room for the media, and even a recording studio.

Joe Amalfitano, now a Dodger coach, served as an infielder with the San Francisco Giants, Chicago Cubs, and
Houston Astros. "I had never seen anything like Dodgertown," he says. "Physically everything here is bigger and
better. And their approach to training is different. There's
such a large crew of instructors that each player, major
or minor leaguer, gets individual attention."

Holman Stadium, in Dodgertown, named for Bud Holman and built in 1953, seats more than six thousand fans.

However, when the Dodgers met the Yankees on March 19, 1979, some 8,200 spectators managed to cram their way into the park.

At Holman Stadium the outfield ends in a grassy embankment that is separated from the field by a low, chain-link fence. When the stadium is sold out, fans are permitted to sit on the embankment to watch the game.

The players' locker room is located about a quarter of a mile from the stadium, and players walk to it. It's easy for fans to intercept the players on their way to or from the stadium for autographs or just a chat.

To keep the players occupied when the day's work is done, Dodgertown offers many different types of recreational facilities. There's a swimming pool, four tennis courts, a movie theater, and two eighteen-hole golf courses. Since the complex also includes plenty of space for conferences, and twelve meeting rooms, the Dodgers rent the facility to companies for business conferences when it's not being used as a training site. As for Holman Stadium, it is used during the summer by the Vero Beach Dodgers of the Florida State League.

At Lakeland, Florida, the Detroit Tigers operate a spring-training complex that is similar to Dodgertown. They call theirs Tigertown.

The club's association with Lakeland is baseball's most enduring spring-training relationship. The Tigers have trained at Lakeland since 1934 except in the World War II years of 1943, 1944, and 1945, when the club traveled to Evansville, Indiana.

There's a closeness between the Tigers and Lakeland, and not merely because their association has lasted so long.

Detroit fans watch the Tigers play at Joker Marchant Stadium in Lakeland, Florida. (George Sullivan)

It also has to do with location. Lakeland is in central Florida, about thirty-five miles east of Tampa, in the heart of the citrus-growing region. There are no beaches nearby, no theme parks. In Lakeland, through much of February and all of March, it's the Tigers and not much else.

The all-concrete Joker Marchant Stadium, named for a former director of parks and recreation in Lakeland, was built in 1967. Many improvements have been made through the years. Check the cars in the parking lot before a game at Marchant Stadium and you're likely to see that Michigan license plates outnumber all others.

Games at Marchant Stadium are almost always sold out, and it's no wonder: It's a joy to watch baseball there. Palm trees surround the park. Country-western music is played between innings. The P.A. announcer is likely to ask everyone to "kindly squeeze a little closer together." And just before the game begins, the announcer gives the sunbaked fans the noontime temperature in Detroit. The colder it is back in Michigan, the louder they cheer and applaud. It's like being at a country fair.

The fans at Joker Marchant Stadium and at other spring-training sites in Florida are mostly old folks, vacationers from the upper Midwest and Northeast. There are many retirees, often married couples. The men wear caps bearing the logo of the teams they root for. The women wear sunglasses and carry seat cushions. There are also college students on their spring breaks and younger kids too, clutching Cokes or boxes of popcorn and programs to be autographed.

Those attending spring-training games also include many of the wives of home-team players. They usually sit directly behind the dugout or close to it. Some of them hold toddlers. During the game fans stop by to greet them. Many take snapshots.

Dodgertown, at Vero Beach, Florida, is unique because it is baseball's only privately-owned spring-training complex. Almost all other spring-training facilities are owned by cities or counties. They have been leased to or simply handed over to the clubs that occupy them.

Toronto Manager Jimy Williams meets the media at the team's
Dunedin, Florida, spring camp.
(George Sullivan)

Cities and counties now realize the value of playing host
to a major league baseball team each spring. The players
and members of a club's administrative staff can be expected to spend at least half a million dollars in the host
city. And that's just the beginning. The media represen-
tatives that cover the team—the newspaper reporters and
photographers, the TV broadcasters and their camera
crews—bring money too.

Most important, there are the tourists that follow the
team. They spend an estimated seven to eight million dollars in hotels, motels, restaurants, and retail shops. For
example, when the Toronto Blue Jays are training at Dun-

edin, Florida, it seems that there are more Canadians than Americans in the local stores and restaurants.

As cities and counties compete for teams, the map of spring training keeps changing. Many of these changes are quite recent, dating from 1985 on. The Houston Astros were unhappy with the facilities they were renting in Cocoa Beach, Florida. They asked the town to spend a few hundred thousand dollars to make some improvements. The town seemed unwilling to do so.

While this was going on, Osceola County, in central Florida, was looking for a way to attract tourists. A baseball team, county officials realized, would do just that. They managed to lure the Astros there with a $5.5 million complex situated between the towns of Kissimmee and St. Cloud that included a 5,200-seat stadium, one of Florida's best, four practice fields, batting cages, and a huge clubhouse with meeting rooms, locker rooms, and dining facilities.

In 1988 *Baseball America* named baseball's top ten spring-training facilities. Osceola County Stadium was ranked first.

Other clubs training in Florida decided they wanted what the Astros had. At the same time, Florida cities and counties realized that they could do what Osceola County had done, and went to work seeking teams. In the next couple of years these changes resulted:

♦ The Texas Rangers moved from Pompano Beach on the east coast to Port Charlotte on the west coast in 1987, occupying a 5,000-seat stadium, four practice diamonds, and modern clubhouses and offices.

The Houston Astros, who train in Kissimmee, Florida, near
Disney World, are visited by Disney characters on opening day.
Catcher is Mark Bailey.
(© Walt Disney Productions, 1985)

◆ The Cincinnati Reds, who had trained in Tampa since 1931, left in 1988, moving twenty-five miles to the east, to Plant City. There they occupied a seven-million-dollar complex that includes four practice fields, four indoor batting cages, and a stadium that seats 6,700.

◆ The Kansas City Royals quit Fort Myers after nine-teen years and landed in a thirteen-million-dollar complex near Haines City, becoming part of the Boardwalk and Baseball amusement park. That was also in 1988. Fans in the 6,500-seat stadium can hear the screams of folks riding the wooden roller coaster. The Royals also have a four-diamond cluster of practice fields, and modern clubhouses and offices. All of the practice fields have the same dimensions as the team's Royals Stadium home.

Boardwalk and Baseball also includes A Taste of Cooperstown, an exhibition of baseball memorabilia and photographs that have been loaned by the National Baseball Hall of Fame. The presentation includes a locker from the New York Yankee clubhouse dating to the time of Babe Ruth.

◆ The New York Mets, also in 1988, abandoned St. Petersburg, where they had shared facilities with the St. Louis Cardinals, in favor of an eleven-million-dollar complex on the other side of Florida in the town of Port St. Lucie. There the Mets have over one hundred acres, with practice fields (one with artificial turf), indoor batting and pitching areas, a huge air-conditioned clubhouse, and a 7,500-seat stadium with the exact dimensions of Shea Stadium.

At Boardwalk and Baseball the infield is artificial turf, but the outfield is the real thing. (Kansas City Royals)

Once these changes were completed, teams occupied these spring-training sites in Florida and Arizona:

Florida Gulf Coast

Seven teams train north and south of Tampa Bay on Florida's Gulf Coast, a region that is also known as the Sun Coast.

Chicago White Sox	Sarasota
Cincinnati Reds	Plant City
Philadelphia Phillies	Clearwater
Pittsburgh Pirates	Bradenton
St. Louis Cardinals	St. Petersburg
Texas Rangers	Port Charlotte
Toronto Blue Jays	Dunedin

Central Florida

Five teams train in central Florida, in an area that is almost midway between the east and west coasts. For fans of these teams who don't want a steady diet of baseball, there are several theme parks in the area. They include Disney World–Epcot Center, Busch Gardens, and Sea World.

Boston Red Sox	Winter Haven
Detroit Tigers	Lakeland
Houston Astros	Kissimmee
Kansas City Royals	Haines City
Minnesota Twins	Orlando

Florida Atlantic Coast

When the New York Mets moved to Port St. Lucie, it brought to six the number of teams that train along the one-hundred-thirty mile strip of Florida's Atlantic Coast. The southernmost site is Miami, where the Orioles are to be found. Vero Beach, where the Dodgers train, is the northernmost site.

As the list below indicates, West Palm Beach is the spring home for two teams—the Braves and Expos. The two share the city's Municipal Stadium.

Atlanta Braves	West Palm Beach
Baltimore Orioles	Miami
Los Angeles Dodgers	Vero Beach
Montreal Expos	West Palm Beach
New York Mets	Port St. Lucie
New York Yankees	Fort Lauderdale

Batting practice for Brian Downing at the Mesa, Arizona, camp
of the California Angels.
(California Angels)

Arizona

Six of the eight teams that train in Arizona—the Cubs,
Angels, Brewers, Mariners, Giants, and Athletics—are
based in Phoenix or near it. The Angels, who train in
Mesa, spend only a month there, switching in mid-March
to a second camp at Palm Springs, California.

The Cleveland Indians are headquartered at Tucson,
which is more than a hundred miles to the south and west
of Phoenix. The San Diego Padres are in Yuma, in the
southwestern corner of the state, only about twenty or so
miles from the Mexican border.

If you enjoy baseball against a backdrop of scattered mountain ranges and vast desert stretches, Arizona is the place to go.

California Angels	Mesa
Chicago Cubs	Mesa
Cleveland Indians	Tucson
Milwaukee Brewers	Chandler
Oakland Athletics	Phoenix
San Diego Padres	Yuma
San Francisco Giants	Scottsdale
Seattle Mariners	Tempe

The 1990s are certain to bring more spring-training switches as Florida cities and counties continue to compete for major league teams, offering vast tracts of lands adorned with new stadiums, practice fields, clubhouses, and all the rest. Even some of the teams that train in Arizona are said to be growing dissatisfied and are listening to offers from Florida communities.

Indeed, each spring there is as much talk about team moves as there is about player trades. The competition for clubs has been described as the hottest game in Florida.

4 ◆ Spring Break

I t was a Sunday morning late in February 1988 at the spring-training headquarters of the Cincinnati Reds, in Plant City, Florida. One batter after another took his turn in the batting cage. Cincinnati Manager Pete Rose looked on.

During a quiet moment infielder Jeff Treadway lashed a ball over third base and into right field.

Rose grinned. "It's good to hear the crack of the bat," he said to no one in particular.

It didn't matter that the field was wet, the sky was gray, the air was cold, and only a sprinkling of fans was on hand. It was the Reds' first spring-training workout of 1988.

To Rose and his veteran players, the superstars especially, it was a good-humored occasion, a time for back slaps and wisecracks.

Indeed, for the team's superstars, it was a typical scene. If you're a superstar, an established player with a million-dollar, multiyear contract, spring training is a pleasant time. There is little stress to it.

In the spring, every day begins with stretching. These are the Philadelphia Phillies. (George Sullivan)

Almost every team has one or two superstars, and some teams have several. There's Wade Boggs of the Red Sox, Rickey Henderson of the Yankees, José Canseco of the Athletics, Darryl Strawberry of the Mets, Tony Gwynn of the Padres, Frank Viola of the Twins, and many more.

Through their talent and skill they have reached the top of the baseball world. Barring serious injury, they are going to be in the lineup when opening day arrives.

They work and sweat and maybe they get their uniforms dirty, but for superstars spring training is usually not difficult. It's something that's necessary, like paying taxes or visiting the dentist. They sharpen their skills. They renew old friendships. But it's a vacation time too. The superstars' biggest worry may be not to get sunburned.

"When you've been at it eight or ten years, spring training is easygoing," says Ozzie Smith, the two-million-a-year shortstop for the St. Louis Cardinals. "There's not a lot of pressure. It's not that difficult, but the day-to-day routine can get monotonous. Whitey [Cardinal Manager Whitey Herzog] just wants each man to be ready for opening day, whatever it takes. Basically, it's up to you.

"If you're established, Whitey routinely gives you a day off each week. I have two sons, ages one and five. We usually make a Disney World trip and one to Busch Gardens. But mostly I like going to a playground and just watching my boys do flips or play on the swings."

Superstars arrive at spring-training camp in first-class physical condition. "It's not like the old days," Whitey Herzog noted in mid-March 1988. "Players didn't make much money and had to hold down off-season jobs. They would sit around too much and show up in Florida with flab hanging over their belts.

"Today's guys make millions. Who needs a winter job? And the players are smart enough to want those big paydays to keep coming. They stay in shape.

"Look at our club. If you see a guy who's fat, it'll be in the wallet."

It's true—the amount of money that players are paid today has had an important impact on conditioning. In 1988 almost a dozen players were earning two million dollars or more for the year. Ozzie Smith of the St. Louis Cardinals, with a salary of $2,340,000, was the game's highest-paid player. Almost eighty players were earning one million a year or more. The average player's salary was approximately $450,000. With that much money at stake, keeping in shape was a year-round activity.

It was different in the past. During the 1950s, when the minimum salary in baseball was $7,500 and players who earned $30,000 or $35,000 a year considered themselves to be handsomely paid, most took jobs during the off-season. It wasn't possible for a player to support himself and his family on his baseball earnings alone.

When spring training arrived, few were in top-flight shape. They had to work hard to get ready for the season.

Players nowadays realize that there's a direct link between being in good condition and how well they perform. Gary Carter, a two-million-a-year star for the New York Mets, is a case in point. In 1987 the 33-year-old Carter had a mediocre season, batting only .235. During the off-season he decided to do something about it. "The first thing I did was say no to a lot of invitations and offers to make appearances," Carter said. "Then I began working with a professional fitness coach."

Carter had a stationary bicycle and several weight-training machines installed in his home. All winter long he worked out several hours a day, five days a week.

Five months later, when he showed up for spring training, he was the talk of the camp. "He's a horse," said Davey Johnson, manager of the Mets. "He's in great shape."

When the regular season got underway, Carter got off to a spectacular start. He was one of the National League's top ten hitters at the end of the first month.

Del Unser, hitting instructor for the Philadelphia Phil-

George Bell, Toronto superstar, tunes up with other Blue Jay outfielders. (George Sullivan)

lies, has kind words for the Phillies, not only because they work hard during the off-season, but also for their insight into what they are doing. "They don't get real bulky muscles," he says. "They keep stretching—which helps in developing long, flexible muscles, the type that track athletes have."

Unser also praises today's players for being sensible about what they eat. "They understand how certain foods give them a tremendous amount of energy," he says. "They avoid fatty foods and things that are high in cholesterol. Many of them have excellent diets."

Nolan Ryan, the superstar pitcher of the Houston Astros, who at the age of forty-one was still throwing the ball as hard as anyone in baseball, was able to do so at least in part because of the attention he paid to diet and exercise. A former Astro trainer called him the "perfect physical specimen" because he took such good care of himself. "I've often eaten with him," said the trainer, "and you can tell by what he orders—so many yellow vegetables, so many green vegetables—that he knows himself well."

Getting in shape to play baseball involves a program with several different parts. Flexibility is vital. Every team encourages players to do stretching exercises to make their muscles limber. In the early weeks of spring training every day begins with stretching.

Strength is another aspect of every fitness program. "Nowadays strength is the name of the game," says Mike Davis, an outfielder for the Oakland Athletics. "Guys like José Canseco [of the A's] or Jesse Barfield [Toronto Blue Jays], they're so strong they can hit the ball out of the park with their hands." Players work on getting stronger through regular Nautilus or free-weight training, or through calisthenics—sit-ups, push-ups, and pull-ups.

Becoming stronger can make a big difference in a player's appearance. When Lenny Dykstra of the New York Mets returned home to Jackson, Mississippi, after the 1987 season, he started working with weights at a local gymnasium. He kept on working right up until it was time to report to camp the next February. By then Dykstra had

Jesse Barfield of the Blue Jays has been hailed for his home-run hands. (George Sullivan)

gained twenty-one pounds, going from 165 to 186.

The added pounds were muscles. The new Dykstra was broad across the chest, heavy in the arms and neck. "Baseball is a strong man's game," he said, "and I wanted to be strong."

Stamina is also vital. Players build heart and lung endurance through running, swimming, cycling, and even by playing such sports as basketball and racquetball.

Many teams have off-season stretching and weight-lifting routines for their players. "Find something you like

to do," says Barry Weinberg, trainer for the Oakland Athletics, "and do it." Several members of the Oakland team keep in shape by playing basketball during the off-season. They might get the same results through a running or stretching program, but basketball is more fun.

The Cincinnati Reds have a very sophisticated fitness program. The club monitors eating, drinking, and sleeping habits. Larry Starr, the Cincinnati trainer, conducts regular tests of body composition—lean muscle versus fat, that is—and of flexibility, strength, and endurance.

"The conditioned athlete competes more often," Starr says. "He's the guy who's going to have a ten- to fifteen-year career."

Once the training season starts, players get to the clubhouse about nine A.M. They take their time dressing. They drink coffee, chat, and read the local newspapers.

In the early weeks of training, practice begins at ten in the morning and lasts until one or one thirty. Players are free to leave then, but there's always the opportunity to do more—for a hitter to work in one of the several batting cages, or for a pitcher to work with a coach and do some throwing.

Infielders never stop taking ground balls. This even applies to Ozzie Smith, the St. Louis Cardinals' exceptional shortstop.

Smith takes as many ground balls as anyone else. "I take a lot of grounders up close," says Smith, "from a guy

Mike Schmidt takes a break during a workout at the Philadelphia training camp. (George Sullivan)

hitting a short distance and hitting relatively hard—not hard to start the spring, but as we go along. It helps my reaction time."

The coach who hits Smith those grounders stands only thirty-five to forty feet away from him. "Right at the cut of the grass," Smith says, "where the grass starts on the infield."

Besides daily on-field drills, Smith works hard on conditioning, particularly weight lifting. At five feet ten, 155 pounds, Smith doesn't have much bulk. Weight lifting, he feels, helps him keep what bulk he does have.

The weight lifting he's done through the years has boosted Smith's endurance. In eight of his first ten seasons, Smith played in ninety-five percent of his team's games. He failed to do so in 1984 because he was hit by a pitch that broke his wrist. In 1985 he was the victim of a deep thigh bruise.

Once the exhibition season begins, games start early in the afternoon and are usually over by four P.M. Many teams play night games, which get underway at seven thirty or eight. They're over by eleven.

Superstars are permitted to follow their own timetables for getting into shape. For example, when Mike Schmidt shows up at the training camp of the Philadelphia Phillies, no one tells him to do this or do that. "We know he'll be prepared on opening day," says Del Unser, hitting instructor for the Philadelphia team. "If his arm's not feeling great one day, he might stress throwing. Other times he works on hitting. It's up to him."

A superstar may play three or four innings of an exhibition game, then decide to call it a day. But some stars who have an opportunity to sit out games don't care to. The New York Yankees' Don Mattingly is one such player. He feels that there is only so much that he can get out of batting-practice sessions and that he needs to hit under game conditions. "I'm anxious to see live pitching," Mattingly declared one spring just before New York's first game of the exhibition season. "I'm ready to put the stuff we've been learning and relearning into practice. These are games with umpires, catchers, no screens in front of the mound; just you and the other guy. When you're hit-

Don Mattingly of the Yankees works hard in the batting cage but needs live pitching to get his swing in shape.
(George Sullivan)

ting off your own pitchers in b.p. [batting practice], you swing at everything. This is a whole different thing."

During spring training each club establishes a local hotel or motel near the stadium as its team headquarters. (These are listed each year in *The National League Green Book* and *The American League Red Book*, available in bookstores.)

All of the rookies and most of the younger players stay at the team hotel, at the team's expense, of course. But a veteran player can choose to accept the rental allowance each team provides and apply that toward accommodations of his own choosing.

Players with families usually bring their wives and children to spring training, and then rent either houses or condominiums. The children, if they're of school age, are entered in local schools or a tutor is hired for them.

"Spring training is probably the most relaxing time of the year as far as the baseball season goes," says Todd Worrell, a relief pitcher for the Cardinals. "At least it is for this organization. I think pretty much everybody on this team brings their families down. Most everyone has a good time."

◇5◇ On the Edge

Spring training may be fun and games for superstars, but for those who are classified as fringe players or marginal players, it is anything but. For such players spring training is very serious business. Every pitch, every at bat, has meaning. Every game has the tension of a World Series game. Futures are at stake.

This situation grows out of the structure of organized baseball, in which the minor leagues, the training ground for future major leaguers, are controlled by the major leagues. Some minor league clubs, or "farm teams," as they're sometimes called, are owned outright by major league clubs. Others have "working agreements" with a club. In either case, the major league club, the "parent" club, supplies the players to the minor club and handles all transactions concerning them.

The minor leagues are classified by the talent level of the players. The highest classification is class AAA. There are four triple A leagues—the American Association, the

A "can't miss" rookie in 1983, Don Mattingly quickly developed into a superstar for the New York Yankees.
(George Sullivan)

International League, the Mexican League, and the Pacific Coast League. In descending order, the other classifications are class AA (three leagues), class A (seven leagues), and, the lowest classification, rookie (three leagues).

In addition, baseball operates an Instructional League for minor league players that have shown the greatest potential. Each major league club has a team in the Instructional League, which begins operation in mid-September with instruction continuing until October 31. Instructional League teams are based at each team's spring-training site.

When a player signs his first professional contract with

a major league team, he becomes the property of that team for a minimum of five years. As the player's skills get sharper and he acquires more experience, he moves up the minor league ladder. He eventually may be offered a major league contract. Upon signing it, he becomes one of forty men the club is allowed to control at any given time.

Of course, the player can be sent back—"optioned"—to a minor league team if he fails to perform as expected. The Yankees transfer young players between Yankee Stadium and their Columbus, Ohio, farm team in the International League with such frequency that the airplane flight between New York and Columbus has been dubbed the Columbus shuttle. Nevertheless, a major league team is permitted to option a player only a limited number of times.

Each team brings its forty players—known as roster players—to spring training. In addition, there are a handful of nonroster players on hand. These are highly promising minor leaguers or free agents whom the manager and coaching staff wish to appraise. These players are known as nonroster invitees.

By April 15, which comes about two weeks after the season begins, the squad must be pared down to twenty-four players. That's the number the team is permitted to carry until September 1, when the major league team can increase its roster to forty players, bringing up additional minor leaguers.

In other words, about half of the players who are on hand during the early weeks of spring training are not going to be around on April 15. At some positions the competition can be fierce. During spring training in 1988 the Indians invited twenty-five pitchers to camp. The club planned to keep only nine or ten. During a span of eleven exhibition games the Toronto Blue Jays used six different third basemen, four different shortstops, and four different second basemen.

Those who feel the tension the most are young players, minor leaguers who have been called up by the parent team and added to its roster. During spring training each of these players must demonstrate that he deserves a promotion. If he fails to do so, he is likely to be sent back to the minors or, worse, released outright.

Most, if not all, of the minor leaguers on the major league roster are classified as rookies. Generally speaking, a rookie is a player who is spending his first year with a major league club. But there is also a technical definition: A rookie is any player who has not batted more than 130 times in the major leagues, pitched fifty innings, or accumulated more than forty-five days on the roster of a major league team.

Every team has one or two rookies who are looked upon as special. These are likely to be players who have been with the organization for two or three years and spent those seasons toiling in the minors. This may be their second or third spring in the major league camp. Everyone now believes they're ready to be promoted. They're given a "can't miss" billing.

In 1983 the "can't miss" rookies included Darryl Straw-

Also labeled "can't miss" in 1983, Buddy Biancalana has missed several times.
(Kansas City Royals)

berry and Don Mattingly. Both had several years of professional experience. Strawberry's career began in 1980 with Kingsport, Tennessee, in the Appalachian League, a rookie league. He did well enough there to be advanced to Lynchburg, Virginia, in the class A Carolina League, where he spent the 1981 season. The next year he played for Jackson, Mississippi, in the class AA Texas League. In 1983 he made the jump to the New York Mets, batting .257 and hitting 26 home runs, capturing Rookie of the Year honors in the National League.

Mattingly's career began in 1979 at Oneonta, New York, in the class A New York–Pennsylvania League. In the years that followed, he played for Greensboro, North Carolina, in the class A South Atlantic League, Nashville in the class A Southern League, and Columbus in the class AAA International League. Mattingly went from Columbus to the Yankees, hitting .283 as a rookie in 1983. He was named the American League's Most Valuable Player in 1985.

In the story of Mike Laga fate played an important role. In 1983, after failing to win a berth on the roster of the Detroit Tigers, Laga was assigned to the club's Evansville, Indiana, farm team in the American Association. He spent not only 1983 there, but also much of 1984. In 1985 he toiled for yet another season in the minors, this time with Nashville, also in the American Association. The following year, 1986, the Tigers traded Laga to the St. Louis Cards.

In the spring of 1988 Laga was labeled "can't miss" one

An exhibition-game injury in 1988 was a painful blow for Mike Laga. (Detroit Tigers; Clifton Boutelle)

more time. By now he had played six years of triple A baseball. He had spent 1987 in the American Association with Louisville, a farm team of the St. Louis Cardinals. There he had batted .304 and smacked 29 home runs.

In spring training in 1988 Laga led the Cards in hitting, home runs, and runs batted in. He seemed certain to win the job of replacing Jack Clark, who had skipped to the Yankees the previous winter. Manager Whitey Herzog said that Laga would be on the St. Louis roster on opening day.

But one March afternoon at Al Lang Stadium in St. Petersburg, only a few weeks before the Cardinals were scheduled to return to St. Louis, misfortune struck. St. Louis was playing Philadelphia. In the fifth inning Laga darted to his left in an attempt to get his glove on Von Hayes's ground ball. "I took a step and my foot came down and hit my glove, a corner of the web," Laga was to say in the locker room afterward. "Because it got caught, I couldn't stand up. So I went right over and landed full-body right on the shoulder. I heard it go r-i-i-i-p! and said, 'What the hell was that?' I looked over and saw the shoulder was kind of lopsided, and decided, 'Well, I'm just going to lie here. I'm not going anywhere.' "

Laga had dislocated his shoulder. When the season opened, Laga was on the disabled list, his career sidetracked once more. A long period of physical rehabilitation lay ahead.

Sometimes a "can't miss" rookie finds his way blocked by a superstar. That's what happened to Randy Milligan, a member of the New York Mets organization. In 1987 Milligan, playing for the Mets' farm team in Tidewater,

Being traded to the Pirates was a happy experience for Randy Milligan. (Pittsburgh Pirates)

hit .326 with 29 home runs and 103 runs batted in and captured the International League's Most Valuable Player award.

Under normal circumstances Milligan would be in line for a promotion. But Milligan had the misfortune to be a first baseman. And the Mets had Keith Hernandez, one of the best first basemen in baseball, at that position.

"It's like a lost cause when you play in back of a guy like Keith," said Milligan, "because no matter what you do or how well you do it you're going to be second best."

It was difficult for the 26-year-old Milligan during spring training in 1988. He didn't want to go back to Tidewater. He had been the International League's MVP the season before. He couldn't improve upon that. Milligan started considering alternatives, like playing in Japan.

"Every time I went out onto the field, I'd be pressing," he said. "I wouldn't be myself. I felt like I had to do something extraordinary to impress the coaches to at least put me on the team as a backup."

Finally the Mets solved the problem for him. Late in March 1988 they traded Milligan to the Pittsburgh Pirates. The door of opportunity had suddenly swung open.

It's not hard to understand why rookie players don't want to be sent back to the minors. Minor league life is not pleasant. The average salary in double A baseball, for example, is only a thousand a month for the seven months of the season, barely enough to survive on.

Most players must buy their own gloves and shoes. Each man receives twelve dollars a day for meals when traveling, which means dining frequently at fast-food restaurants.

Games are played exclusively at night, often under lights so dim the outfielders have trouble seeing fly balls. And there are bus trips between league cities that stretch for many hundreds of miles on unfamiliar roads. "It's stupid," says one veteran player. "You travel fourteen hours on a bus, and *then* you're supposed to play baseball."

Most players find there is little fun to playing minor league ball. In college or high school you play for a team. You want the team to win. In the minors you still feel that way, but not as much. Everyone is trying to make the big leagues. There's much more of an emphasis on individual performance as a result. "If the team does well," says another veteran, "and you don't, well, you don't feel so good."

The truth is that only about ten percent of all minor leaguers ever advance to the majors. And after a season or two every player knows whether he is in that ten percent or just filling out the lineup, toiling away at a game he loves but for about the same amount of money he could earn back home at a McDonald's.

In 1988 there was an opening on the roster of the New York Mets for infielder Keith Miller, who, although he had played a few games for the team, was a minor leaguer. Miller's role with the Mets was to be that of a backup player, which meant he wouldn't be playing very often, only when one of the regulars was injured or otherwise out of the lineup. For long stretches the chances were good he would not play at all.

Did that bother him? Not at all. He was delighted with the promotion. "I want to stay very much," he said. That's exactly the way any minor leaguer would have felt.

Just as spring training is a time of great stress for rookie players, so it is for those veterans whose best seasons are already in the record book. But instead of being faced with a trip to the minor leagues and perhaps the opportunity to try out again the next year, the veteran may be facing the end of a career.

Pitcher Tommy John, often referred to as an "aging left-hander," knows what that feels like. Released by the Oakland A's in 1985 after having won 259 games in a career that covered twenty-two seasons, John was invited to spring training in 1986 by the New York Yankees.

Nobody gave him much of a chance of making the club. He was handed a uniform with number sixty-five on the back. Numbers that high are usually worn by only the most lightly regarded of prospects.

But after spring training John was wearing his familiar twenty-five; he had made the team.

"Spring training is a funny creature," John has said. "You like to use it to get yourself ready for the season,

Tommy John (left, with Don Mattingly), who celebrated his 44th birthday in 1987, a year he won thirteen games for the Yankees, was one of baseball's most durable players.
(George Sullivan)

but you can't do that if you have to make the team.

"In other words, you can't work on the pitches you have to work on for the season because you have to get batters out. I'm basically a two-pitch pitcher—fastball, curveball. So in spring training I like to work on my off-speed pitches. Of course, you can work on them, but you can't work on them in a game, not if you're trying to make the team.

"Every outing has to be a good outing. If you don't have a good outing, you're history."

John's career continued through 1987, when he won

thirteen games and was the Yankees' most durable pitcher, and into 1988. On May 22 of that year John celebrated his forty-fifth birthday. "You have to accept the fact that you are physically less than you were at twenty-two or -three," said John, "but I also know that I can pitch a whole lot better now than I did then."

Not every attempt to extend a career is as successful as Tommy John's was. Joe Cowley, a 29-year-old pitcher with the Philadelphia Phillies, went to spring training in 1988 fully aware his career was in hanging by a thread. A pitcher with a 32–19 record in four seasons in the American League, Cowley in 1987 had suddenly lost the ability to put the ball in the strike zone. In five games, in which he had pitched only eleven and two thirds innings, Cowley had given up twenty-one hits and walked seventeen.

The Phillies sent Cowley to a minor league team, the Maine Guides of the International League. Things kept going downhill. In sixty-three innings Cowley gave up sixty-three hits and walked seventy-six. That July, Cowley and the Phillies decided it would be a good idea for him to quit and start again the next year.

Before spring training in 1988 Cowley went to the University of Tennessee to work with Mark Conner, the baseball coach. Conner had been the pitching coach for the Yankees during a period that Cowley had spent with the New York team. "We worked on certain mechanics, something to do with the hips," Cowley said. "He got my confidence up."

The Phillies invited Cowley to spring training as a non-roster player. The club hoped that he would be able to find the strike zone again.

Joe Cowley poses with Philadelphia strength coach Gus Hoe-
fling at spring-training camp in 1988.
(George Sullivan)

Cowley was filled with anxiety the first time he pitched.
"I knew everybody and their brother was watching me,"
he said.

Cowley's performances were mostly sad. In one inning
against Toronto, Cowley gave up three runs on four walks
and a hit. Against Los Angeles a few days later he loaded

the bases with walks but managed to pitch out of the inning. In seven innings, he walked ten batters and hit two.

Cowley's attempt at a comeback didn't last a full month. In mid-March the Phillies released him. When no other team sought his services, Cowley knew his career was over.

There are twenty-six major league teams. There are twenty-four players to a team. That figures out to 624 jobs. Before spring training opens, most of them are already filled by holdover players. Rookies and aging veterans scramble for what's left. "If you don't like it," observed veteran pitcher Paul Mirabella in the spring of 1988, "you do something else."

6 ◇ Minor Leaguers

At modern-day spring-training complexes, players on the major league roster and the various minor league teams train at the same site. They do, however, have separate clubhouses and practice fields.

They do not live together either. Major league players stay at the team hotel or rent apartments or houses. Minor leaguers often live in dormitories within the spring-training site.

Even though a team may have two or three hundred minor league players on hand, no one is anonymous. Thanks to computerized performance records, plus detailed reports from the Instructional League and the winter leagues in Latin America, managers know about what to expect from each of the minor league players in their organizations.

One or two of the minor leaguers may be in line for promotion to the parent team; they're "can't miss" rookies. But the majority of minor leaguers realize that the most

Jack Morris, a graduate of Tigertown, gets ready for an exhibition game appearance at Joker Marchant Stadium in Lakeland. (George Sullivan)

they can hope for is to be advanced to a minor league team with a higher classification.

They work hard. They strive to make themselves visible. But they're ready to accept their fate.

"Realistically, I know there's not much of a chance of my making the team," said Jay Buhner, a young outfielder the Yankees invited to camp in the spring of 1987. "But you never know. You could have a great spring and have an outside chance. Maybe somewhere down the line they'll think of me."

Minor league players under contract to the Detroit Tigers train at Tigertown, the same Lakeland, Florida, site used by the major league team. They live in a three-story, air-conditioned dormitory named John E. Fetzer Hall. Mr. Fetzer is the club's chairman of the board of directors.

Tigertown is something like a summer camp for boys. Only these "boys" all happen to be from eighteen to twenty-one years old. And most are about the size of pro football linebackers, standing six feet and taller and weighing at least two hundred pounds.

Dormitory rooms are simply furnished. Each has two beds, two chairs, two good-sized lockers, a nightstand, and

At Tigertown, John E. Fetzer Hall is the home for minor league players. (George Sullivan)

a writing desk. The showers and bathroom are down the hall. Neither women nor alcoholic beverages are permitted in the rooms.

On a typical day the minor league players are awakened at seven thirty, and then have breakfast in the Tigertown dining hall. At one end of the room is a huge photo mural depicting championship Tiger teams of the past.

The players are out on the practice fields at ten A.M. for two and a half hours of instruction and drills. After lunch there's more instruction, more drills. By mid afternoon the workouts are over. For recreation most players golf or fish. If the Tigers happen to be playing a game at Marchant Stadium that day, the minor leaguers watch from the stands.

In recent years such players as Jack Morris, often named baseball's outstanding pitcher of the 1980s, and infielder Alan Trammel, twice voted Tiger of the Year, are among the players who have come through the Tigers' minor league system. "You can tell the real players, the ones who want to make something out of themselves," says Tom Gallo, one of the two dormitory night clerks. "They get to their meals on time. They're in their rooms at ten o'clock. They don't drink or chase women.

"And they're not afraid to work. They take extra batting and fielding practice."

What surprises Gallo is how few of the young players take advantage of the opportunity that Tigertown offers. "To a lot of guys it's a vacation," Gallo says. "Only about twenty-five percent of them really work. They're the ones that eventually make it."

Twenty-three-year-old Hector Berrios, a left-handed

pitcher, was one of the young hopefuls with the Detroit Tigers in the spring of 1988. Raised in New York City's borough of the Bronx not far from Yankee Stadium, Berrios spent the 1987 season with a Tiger farm team, the Fayetteville (North Carolina) Generals of the class A South Atlantic League.

"I made a good showing," he said. "I was seven and seven. But I had a two point nine ERA [earned run average], and for every inning I pitched, I struck out at least one batter, which shows I had a good arm.

"I was throwing the ball at eighty-seven miles an hour," said Berrios, who first played baseball as a Little Leaguer in New York's Central Park. "I was throwing strikes. That really impressed them."

Because of his success, the Tigers moved Berrios up the ladder a couple of rungs. He was offered a contract with the Toledo Mud Hens of the International League, a triple A league.

"I just take one day at a time," said Berrios, who was a star player at James Monroe High School in the Bronx. "I just work hard every day. I try not to let myself get distracted.

"Some guys come here and treat it like a vacation. You can't do that. You have to be like a boxer getting ready for a fight. Everything else is secondary.

"You have to have confidence, too—a lot of confidence. And you have to be able to apply all the things they teach you.

"When you can do all these things together, you shouldn't have too rough a time of it. The only thing ahead of you is the major leagues."

Hector Berrios watches the Tigers' preseason competition at Joker Marchant Stadium. (George Sullivan)

Berrios looked forward to pitching batting practice against the Tigers before the spring training ended. He grinned at the prospect of throwing curves and fastballs to such veteran players as Chet Lemon and Alan Trammel.

Toronto hitting instructor John Mayberry (left) welcomes young Junior Felix, newly arrived from the Dominican Republic, to the Blue Jays' training camp in 1988. (George Sullivan)

"Maybe I'll impress [Detroit Manager] Sparky Anderson," he said. "Maybe he'll start keeping an eye on me."

Some minor leaguers undergo more than the normal amount of stress. These are Latin American players. For many of them spring training in Florida or Arizona represents their first trip away from home, their first brush with American culture. It can be difficult. "It's real tough," says Chicago White Sox pitcher Fred Manrique, who was born in Venezuela and returns there when the baseball season ends in October. "You're so homesick, you want to cry."

A survey conducted by the *St. Petersburg Times* revealed there were 113 players from Latin America on major league rosters in 1988. That's slightly more than ten percent of all players. These players come chiefly from the Dominican Republic, Puerto Rico, and Venezuela.

"Latino kids are just like other kids," says Winston Llenas, a native of Santiago in the Dominican Republic and a coach for the Toronto Blue Jays. "They want to be in the big leagues.

"The leagues there aren't as organized as here, but the level of play is just as good. Baseball is like a religion there. Everybody's goal is to come here and play."

St. Louis Cardinal catcher Tony Peña, also from the Dominican Republic, remembers how it was when he came to the United States for the first time in 1976. He knew he was going to be lonely, but he didn't realize how lonely until he had his first meal. "I looked around and my family wasn't there," he recalls. "I looked at the plate, and I didn't recognize the foods. It was very, very hard. You get sick mentally, and it hurts your game."

Toronto Blue Jay outfielder George Bell, the American League's Most Valuable Player of the 1987 season, is from the Dominican Republic too. As a young boy he dreamed of coming to the United States "to be like Babe Ruth," he says. He started hitting balls with sugarcane sticks at the

George Bell of the Blue Jays, from the Dominican Republic, was the American League's MVP in 1987. (George Sullivan)

age of seven. He was playing baseball seriously at fourteen. By the time George had finished high school, his name was well known by the scouts who crisscrossed the Dominican Republic representing major league teams.

Bell was seventeen when he signed with Toronto for a $3,500 bonus. Shortly after, he arrived in the United States for the first time. Although he knew a little English, he refused to talk with reporters because he didn't want to "look stupid." In the clubhouse, when players and coaches made jokes and laughed, Bell would laugh too, even though he didn't know what he was laughing at.

Says Bell about those days: "Even though I was on the baseball field, my favorite place to be, I was sad."

Bell, like most other Latin American players, eventually overcame the sadness. But as his experience indicates, it sometimes requires more than the ability to hit and catch a baseball to become a major leaguer. It also requires determination and the ability to turn aside loneliness.

7 Getting Pitchers Ready

The scene is Chain O' Lakes Park in Winter Haven, Florida, home grounds of the Boston Red Sox each spring. It is seven thirty in the morning. Workouts and practice begin at ten.

The clubhouse doors are locked. The stands are empty.

Out in the field, beyond second base, somebody is running, and running hard. He has been at it for almost an hour. His sweatshirt and shorts are drenched with sweat.

That somebody is Roger Clemens, one of baseball's top pitchers, winner of the American League's Cy Young Award in 1986 and 1987. During spring training Clemens runs hard almost every day.

After he's pushed himself about as far as he can, he takes a shower, changes into his uniform, and starts regular practice with the rest of the players.

Roger Clemens is not atypical. Pitchers work harder than any other group of players to get in shape. Even superstar pitchers can't escape the grind.

"Your legs are especially important," says Clemens. "I've

Pitchers run—and run and run. These are New York Met hurlers at St. Lucie, Florida.
(Copyright 1988, New York Mets; Gina Minielli)

got three leg machines and an arm machine in my garage at home. I spend two hours working out every day."

Strength is what gives Clemens stamina. "When people are tiring out late in the year, I can turn it on," he says. "I like to start strong and finish strong."

Pitchers do so much running that they get weary of it. "I hate running," says 38-year-old Bob Forsch of the St. Louis Cardinals. "But I know if I want to keep pitching, I've got to run."

Sparky Anderson, manager of the Detroit Tigers, uses a special drill to get pitchers to do their running. Sparky gathers the pitchers in a cluster in left center field. Sparky stands by himself in right center. One by one the pitchers

Roger Clemens of the Red Sox, the American League's Cy Young award winner in 1986 and 1987, following his twentieth victory in 1987.
(Aime LaMontagne)

run toward Sparky at half speed. As each man goes past, he flips Sparky a ball, then starts running at full tilt, as if he were a wide receiver running straight downfield for a forward pass. Sparky sends the baseball arcing in the pitcher's direction. The pitcher makes the catch, then jogs back to the group to await his turn again.

The drill makes a game out of running for the pitchers. It also enables Sparky to keep his arm in shape.

At the same time they're running to build their stamina, the pitchers are also working to get their arms in shape. "Every man has to work hard," says 48-year-old Claude Osteen, who in 1988 began his seventh season as the pitching coach for the Philadelphia Phillies. "No matter how much work they've done before they come to camp, it's going to take so many pitches, so many laps of running, so much fielding at first base—all the routines we go through—to make a guy's arm come around.

"Fans can sit in the stands and see a pitcher throw the ball," says Osteen. "But they don't know whether the guy has his good fastball, whether the ball is live or not. It just takes so many innings of pitching to bring that about."

From the first day of camp Osteen, who won 196 games as a major leaguer and pitched in two World Series, has every pitcher throwing. They throw the ball relatively slowly at first, increasing speed day by day.

Pitchers and catchers are the first players to arrive at training camp. After the pitchers have been throwing for a couple of weeks, the other players arrive. Pitchers then begin throwing batting practice. "Each pitcher," says Osteen, "will probably throw three or four sessions of batting practice before playing any games."

Once the exhibition games begin, all of the pitchers on Osteen's staff have to be available to work. "That's when we start stretching pitchers out," he says. "You're no longer working on just getting the arm in shape. You

start working on pitches, on control, on movement. You start working on delivery, which is a big thing."

Osteen also helps in developing new pitches. "If a pitcher needs time to come up with something new," he says, "spring training is the time to work on it, the time to experiment."

Dave Stieb, a 30-year-old right-hander on the staff of the Toronto Blue Jays, uses spring training to develop his basic pitches—his fastball, curve, and slider.

His first appearance of the 1988 exhibition season was no triumph. The Cincinnati Reds rocked Stieb for four earned runs in two and one third innings. Several days later he was better, pitching four shutout innings against the St. Louis Cardinals, striking out two, walking none.

"The first outing I basically just threw the fastball mixed with a slider and curve," said Stieb. "The next time I was throwing the curve pretty good."

In his third spring outing Stieb had another good showing. He struck out four in five innings of work in Toronto's 5–3 win over the Philadelphia Phillies.

"Everything is pretty much on schedule," Stieb said after the game. "I'm trying to find a consistent delivery to aid keeping the ball down. The slider was going where I wanted it to until the last inning, when I knew I was about done and I tried to throw too hard."

Getting one's arm in shape is not only a long process, it is a painful one. Says Osteen: "Pitching in a game, with all the pressure and tension a pitcher puts on himself, is

Philadelphia pitching coach Claude Osteen toils to get his arm in shape. (George Sullivan)

different than pitching batting practice or doing any other type of pitching. And no matter how well conditioned a pitcher is, his arm is going to get sore after a game."

Pain is a tremendous problem with pitchers who suffer from adhesions. These occur when tissues in the arm and shoulder that are normally not connected join together during the winter when the arm is being rested. "These adhesions have to be broken down," says Osteen. "Otherwise your good stuff is not going to come."

It doesn't happen overnight. "Sometimes it takes two thirds of the way through spring training before the adhesions are broken down and the pain begins to lessen.

"It can hurt, really hurt, to throw," says Osteen. "But you have to keep working, keep exercising."

When it comes to pain, Osteen speaks from personal experience. As a coach, he pitches batting practice every day during the regular season. So in spring training he has to work, just as the members of his staff do, to get his arm back in shape.

"You can't imagine what we go through," he says. "It hurts. Believe me, *it hurts*. But you have to put up with it. It's part of the process."

In recent years the Phillies, like many other teams, have been using videotape to help improve pitcher performance. "Every game in the spring is tape recorded," says Osteen. "We study it constantly."

Osteen says that videotape is a big help. "You tell a pitcher what you think he's doing that's wrong, tell him

Oakland's Storm Davis bears down during preseason outing at Phoenix Stadium. (Oakland Athletics)

what you're seeing. And then you can take him into the film room and play the tape and freeze the frame—stop it dead—and show him exactly what the problem is. The tape supports what you're telling him.

"It used to be that you'd tell a pitcher what you thought he was doing wrong, and he'd sometimes deny it. 'I'm not doing that,' he'd say. Well, now you can show him what he's doing; he can see for himself."

During spring training in 1988, when Dwight Gooden, ace pitcher for the New York Mets, was having problems with his delivery, pitching coach Mel Stottlemyre showed him a videotape of one of his outstanding pitching performances in the spring of 1986. Then Stottlemyre showed Gooden a tape of one of his spring-training games in 1988. "The difference was like night and day," Gooden said.

From viewing the two tapes, the New York pitcher saw that he was not getting the rhythm and drive that had enabled him to use his body to propel the ball when he threw. He had let himself become an "arm" pitcher.

In his next outing Gooden turned his body more on each pitch. This helped him to get more pushing action from his right leg. He began throwing a more lively fastball. In a game against the Minnesota Twins, Gooden pitched six scoreless innings, allowing only two hits. Stottlemyre clocked Gooden's fastball at ninety-five miles per hour, which is superstar speed.

Claude Osteen, like other pitching coaches, also works with minor league players during the training season. The Phils have minor league teams in the triple A International League, in the Eastern League (AA), Florida State League

Seattle pitching coach Billy Connors (left) has some tips for minor league prospect Terry Taylor at the Mariners' camp in Tempe, Arizona. (Seattle Mariners)

(A), South Atlantic League (A), New York–Penn League (A), and in the rookie leagues.

"We might bring in some pitchers from the minor league camp to throw batting practice," Osteen says. "Or we might need a couple of extra guys to pitch for us in a B game [see page 106]. That's when I get to know the minor leaguers."

When Philadelphia's spring-training camp opened in

Pitching coach Al Widmar has advice for Toronto hurlers at the club's Dunedin, Florida, training camp. (George Sullivan)

1988, Osteen had nineteen pitchers on his staff. The club planned to open the season with a ten-man staff. That meant that nine pitchers were going to have to be assigned to minor league teams or released outright.

"It's usually the manager [Lee Elia] who tells a player he's going to be sent to the minors," says Osteen. "But a lot of times he'll ask me to sit in with him.

"We try to be positive, try to give the player some good, solid reason why he's being sent down.

"Sometimes going to the minors is the best thing. For instance, at the beginning of the season there are a lot of off days. That's the way the schedule is arranged; plus there are postponements because of bad weather. What this means is that you usually don't need a fifth starting pitcher until after the first month of the season. So if we have a young pitcher who we plan to make the fifth starter, he's better off in the minor leagues, getting three or four starts under his belt. He won't be doing any good for himself sitting on the bench in the major leagues, just watching things. We can call him up when we need him.

"When we sit with a young player and explain things like that, he leaves here in a much better frame of mind than he would otherwise."

Once spring training ends, Osteen and other pitching coaches continue to work with their pitchers on a daily basis. "You get to know each man inside and out," Osteen

Dodger pitcher Orel Hershiser dashes from the mound to cover first as other Dodger pitchers look on.
(© Los Angeles Dodgers, 1985)

says. "You've got to be like a mother hen to them. You have to be a psychologist maybe even more than a teacher.

"You're constantly watching their deliveries, looking for something that might go wrong. Sometimes during the season a problem will develop, a tight spot in a pitcher's shoulder, maybe a kink—something that causes him to alter his delivery. You're always on the lookout for things like that."

◆8◆ Working on Hitting

One mid-March morning at Municipal Stadium in West Palm Beach, Atlanta Braves outfielder Dale Murphy, one of the outstanding home-run hitters of the 1980s, showed up twenty minutes late for batting practice. He had been delayed because he had locked his keys in his car.

"Why'd you bother showing up?" a teammate shouted. "You don't need b.p."

Murphy grinned, put on a helmet, grabbed his bat, and entered the batting cage the moment it was his turn. He swung hard at each of twelve pitches, missing none of them.

Afterward he said, "No matter how many home runs you hit, you can never stop practicing. As soon as you think you've mastered something, that's when you start slipping."

Batting practice—or b.p., as the players call it—is serious business. No player would think of going a single day without hitting against "live" pitching.

Yankees' Rickey Henderson unlimbers for a session in the batting cage. (George Sullivan)

Even pitchers work on their hitting—at least, National League pitchers do. Pitchers in the American League don't have to give hitting much thought. That's because in the American League a designated hitter takes the pitcher's batting turn.

In batting practice a pitcher throws from a regulation mound. He's shielded from line drives by a protective screen that stands on the down slope of the pitchers' mound.

The batter takes his stance in a steel-mesh cage. Several other players are gathered around the cage, each awaiting his turn.

Usually the batter loosens up by first hitting line drives

to the opposite field. (For a right-handed hitter, whose nature it is to pull the ball to left field, the opposite field is right field.) Then he'll drive the ball up the middle and into left field.

The team's hitting coach or instructor frequently stands behind the cage and watches carefully. He designates how many swings each batter is to take.

Hitters don't go up there to swing away in meaningless fashion. The coach will often set up a strategic situation. He may say, for instance, "Man on third, no outs." That means the hitter is to hit a long fly ball, giving a phantom base runner a chance to tag up and score.

Or the coach may say, "Two bunts; five swings, hit and

Before batting practice, Detroit's Ray Knight has a word with hitting coach Vada Pinson. (George Sullivan)

run." That instructs the hitter to bunt the first two pitches, then attempt to drive the ball to the right side in an effort to advance the runner on first.

At the same time that batting practice is going on, other coaches are hitting practice fly balls and grounders—fungoes—to outfielders and infielders. A coach tosses a ball into the air, then hits it with a special fungo bat, a bat with a long, thin handle and short, thick head.

The fungo bat enables the ball to be placed with pinpoint accuracy. The coach doing the hitting can send an outfielder to his right or left, or force him to go back or come forward. Some coaches have the ability to fungo a

Toronto Manager Jimy Williams, one of baseball's many skilled fungo hitters. (George Sullivan)

Bob Knepper of the Astros faces a robot pitcher.
(Osceola County Stadium and Sports Complex; Loretta
Lombardy)

ball straight up in the air. That kind of fungo enables a
catcher to practice gloving high pops.

No one is certain where the word "fungo" comes from.
Dickson's Dictionary of Baseball says the word dates to 1867
and may have been created simply by combining the words
"fun" and "go."

Hitters also tune up their swings against robot pitchers.
There are several at each camp. About the size of a home
dishwasher, the robot pitcher is a mechanical contraption
that can fire baseballs at speeds of up to a hundred miles
an hour. And keep firing them. The robot pitcher's "arm"
never tires. The machine never asks for a day off. It has
no agent and draws no salary.

Not only does a robot never get weary, it throws a

Mechanical pitches can be ordered in countless variations. (George Sullivan)

greater variety of pitches and throws them harder than any real pitcher. It has a fastball, a flat curve, a dropping curve, a flat slider, and a dropping slider. A mechanical pitcher costs about two thousand dollars.

The robot is placed at one end of a rectangular net enclosure. At the other end there's a plate. The batter stands at the plate while a coach rolls balls one by one down a metal chute toward two small rubber wheels that are mounted on their sides. The wheels, driven by a motor, are spinning in opposite directions. The wheels seize each ball as it reaches the end of the chute and fires it toward the batter. By tilting the machine to the left or right, and by varying the revolutions per minute of each of the wheels, different types of pitches can be thrown.

The purpose of the robot is to enable batters to get loose at the plate, toughen their hands, and find their batting rhythms.

Sometimes a robot will be used to help a hitter overcome a weakness. If, for example, a hitter has a problem with the slider down and away, the machine is adjusted accordingly. Then the hitter can spend as much time as he wants facing nothing but sliders down and away. A pitching machine is good for practicing bunting, too.

Earlier robots were not as sophisticated. Each was equipped with a metal arm that swung up and over to rifle the ball toward the plate. But the pitch was always a fastball. There was no way to get the machine to make the ball curve.

Most players feel that hitting against machines has only limited value, no matter how talented the robot happens to be. The hitter eventually gets used to seeing the same pitch over and over. He can time his swing and smack it. Players agree that live pitching offers greater opportunity for improvement.

Hitters also have the opportunity to hit from a batting tee during spring training. The tee is a length of rubber tubing, the height of which can be adjusted, upon which the ball is placed.

Sometimes batters use the batting tee in an effort to school themselves to hit down. Swinging down slightly is what most coaches recommend. When the ball is struck with a downward swing, it flies off the bat with an upward spin, which makes it climb. Home runs are the result of hitting down. Hank Aaron, who hit more home runs than anyone else in major league history, never swung up.

Every team has a special coach or instructor to work with hitters. What the coaches do isn't limited to spring training, however. A hitting coach is on the job twelve months a year.

Del Unser, hitting instructor for the Philadelphia Phillies, keeps in touch with the team's hitters by telephone during the off-season. "I give most of them a call," he says. "There are usually a couple of guys I'm concerned about. I want to be sure they're on a winter conditioning program and they don't get heavy."

When it comes to sharpening their batting skills during the off-season, some players hit off batting tees in their garages or basements. They may do this three or four times a week, says Unser. It helps their timing. Other players get hitting practice by working out with high school or college teams in their area.

Once players arrive at camp, they hit off pitching machines. This strengthens their hands and also helps with their timing.

"Then they hit off of hard-throwing pitchers," Unser says. "And they hit off the coaches, who don't throw so hard.

"All of this helps them to get their timing. We really stress timing."

As the Philadelphia hitting instructor, Unser, who played for five different teams, the Phillies included, in his fifteen-year major league career, studies each hitter as he takes his turn in the batting cage. He talks to many of them, offering suggestions.

Jim Olander of the Phillies tees off.
(George Sullivan)

Hitting instructor Del Unser (left, with coach Tony Taylor) played for the Indians, Mets, and Expos before landing with the Phillies. (George Sullivan)

What Unser would like to do is make every Philadelphia .230 hitter a .260 hitter, and every .260 hitter a .300 hitter. To improve, perhaps a hitter has to learn to hit to the opposite field.

Well, Unser may advise the man to shift his feet to go to the right, or swing with quicker hand movement.

Most hitters today follow one of two basic theories. One is based on the teachings of Charley Lau, who coached the hitters of the Kansas City Royals for many years. In instructing the Royals, and in his book, *The Art of Hitting*

.300, Lau taught the discipline of the head and the importance of shifting weight. Two of today's best hitters, Wade Boggs of the Red Sox and Don Mattingly of the Yankees, practice what Lau preached.

One of baseball's all-time greats, Ted Williams, who won six batting titles and, with a .406 average in 1941, was the last player to hit .400, disagrees with Lau's theories. He says that "Lau may have set back hitting twenty-five years." Williams stresses the discipline of the hips in hitting. He set down what he believed in *The Science of Hitting*. First published more than twenty years ago, the book is still popular.

"Ted Williams was not much on the mechanics of hitting, the actual swing," says Unser. "He believed that you had to have a slight uppercut, which almost everyone does have."

But Unser says that hitting slightly up is essentially having a level swing. "That's because the ball is coming from a down angle from the pitchers' mound."

Unser differs with Williams in that he wants the Philadelphia hitters to swing "slightly down and through, as well and as firmly as possible."

Unser hails Williams as "probably the greatest at figuring out what pitches he was going to hit in certain situations.

"He really knew what they were trying to do to him," Unser says.

Unser wants the Philadelphia hitters to have that kind of discipline—to take pitches, waiting for a good pitch to hit. "You don't become great without discipline," he says.

A few players don't need any instruction from coaches

Unser in a frequent pose inspects a Philadelphia hitter.
(George Sullivan)

or very much work on their hitting during spring training. That's because they have played winter baseball in such places as Venezuela, the Dominican Republic, and Puerto Rico. But just about everyone else except the pitchers goes to spring training to concentrate on hitting. The players spend hours each day swinging the bat. It is recognized that even a poorly conditioned player can get base hits if his skill level is high.

◇9◇ Spring Games

Willie McGee of the St. Louis Cardinals laced the ball down the third-base line just over the base. Fair or foul? Obviously it was fair, for it kicked up a puff of white chalk dust as it skipped toward the outfield.

"Foul!" cried the umpire without a second's hesitation.

There was no argument from the Cardinals. McGee returned to the plate.

In the St. Louis clubhouse after the game, won by the Toronto Blue Jays, 5–3, Cardinal Manager Whitey Herzog discussed the play. He described the ball that McGee hit as being "right on the chalk."

Why didn't he argue, a reporter wanted to know. Was it because it was a mere exhibition game and didn't count?

Herzog grinned. "I never argue with a woman," he said, "except my wife."

A woman? A woman behind home plate? A woman umpire?

Bob Knepper of the Astros swings in vain during preseason game at Osceola County Stadium.
(Osceola County Stadium and Sports Complex)

Yes. In spring training in 1988 a female umpired a full schedule of games.

Her name: Pam Postema. That spring Postema was one of seven umpires given a chance to compete for two vacancies on the National League's umpiring staff.

Postema, at the age of thirty-three, was organized baseball's only female umpire. But she was no newcomer to the game. After graduating from umpire school in 1977, she made steady progress toward the top of her profession. Her experience included five years in triple A baseball—one year in the American Association and four in the Pacific Coast League.

Her experience also included having her collarbone broken by a high fastball a young catcher could not hold and her toe broken by a foul tip. She had been spit at, sworn at, and called names.

"She's not here because she's a female," Ed Vargo, supervisor of umpires for the National League, told *Sports Illustrated*. "She's here because she has gotten good recommendations from minor league managers and from our people who scouted her."

Earlier that spring Postema worked a weekend series between the Atlanta Braves and the Montreal Expos at West Palm Beach. "I thought she was very good," said Chuck Tanner, former manager of the Braves. "She called third strikes without hesitation. She called a balk on my guy, and it was a balk. You don't even notice after an inning or two. She's an umpire."

Postema never made a big deal about being baseball's only female umpire. "I don't want to be a cause," she said. "I umpire because I love the game and it's a challenge."

Late in March 1988, Postema was told she wasn't going to be promoted. Two other umpires were being named to fill the openings.

When the major league season opened in 1988, Postema was working in the American Association. A spokesperson for the National League said she would be invited back for major league spring training in 1989.

Spring training games look like the games you see during the regular season. There are nine players on a side, and base runners try to score runs. But there are some differences. Having a female umpire behind the plate or working the base paths is only one of them.

During the regular season teams play to win. In spring training they play to win too, but not every minute. There may be some other things managers want to do.

For example, a pitcher who has pitched two or three shutout innings and has given up, say, one or two hits and not walked anybody—a pitcher who is being dominating—will suddenly be replaced by an inexperienced rookie who will quickly hand the opposition some runs.

It's not that the manager isn't thinking about winning the game. It's simply that he is more concerned about getting all his pitchers' arms in shape. Several pitchers are likely to see action in every game.

In a preseason game a superstar may take a turn or two at bat, then be succeeded by a pinch hitter. The superstar doesn't remain on the bench. He's got the afternoon off. He goes to the clubhouse, showers, dresses, and heads for the golf course.

As these paragraphs suggest, exhibition games aren't taken quite as seriously as those played during the regular season. During a preseason game you might see players from one team or another running wind sprints in the outfield. If this happened during the regular season, it would cause a furor. The umpires would stop the game, and the jogging players would be ordered from the field. But in exhibition games they're scarcely noticed.

During the regular season, games that are tied after nine innings continue to be played until one team has more

Players jog in the outfield during a Red Sox game at Joker Marchant Stadium. (George Sullivan)

runs than the other, no matter how many innings it may take. But in spring training opposing managers usually agree, in the event of a tie, to play no more than nine or ten innings.

Nine or ten innings is all that it is going to take to accomplish what each wants to that day. There's no good reason to play additional innings and risk tiring players.

Fans don't seem to mind that games are occasionally played to no decision. After all, it's spring training.

League rules forbid players from one team from associating with players from the opposition team before a game. But in spring training these rules are relaxed. Players, coaches, and managers often chat and joke during batting practice, and no one seems to mind.

Contests in Florida are often preceded by ceremonies

Detroit catcher Matt Nokes takes time out for family matters during late innings of an exhibition game at the team's Lakeland, Florida, training base. (George Sullivan)

of different types. Sometimes the local mayor and various city commissioners get introduced.

Before a game between the Phillies and Tigers at Clearwater's Jack Russell Stadium one March Saturday, the pregame show was a wedding. Three years after their first date there, Tammy Palmer, twenty-six, and Chris English, twenty-nine, both computer technicians, exchanged vows behind home plate.

After, the couple kissed as the spectators cheered. Then they walked to their bleacher seats, smiling and waving.

One fan was not impressed. The moment the ceremony ended, he shouted out, "Play ball!"

Team wins and losses in the Grapefruit and Cactus leagues are recorded in a combined standings for both leagues. Games in which a major league team opposes a minor league or college team do not count in the standings. Nor do games involving "B" teams, with fifteen or twenty players on each. For example, the Philadelphia A team might play the Detroit Tigers, while the Phillies' B team takes on the St. Louis Cardinals. Splitting the squads in this fashion—each team, in fact, is known as a split squad—gives more players a chance to play.

Daily newspapers keep track of the standings of the teams in the Grapefruit and Cactus Leagues. But there is

For an exhibition game against the Cardinals early in March 1988, Philadelphia manager Lee Elia made out this A-team lineup. (Philadelphia Phillies)

#				#		
1	Stone	7 ●		1	Coleman	
2	Thompson	8	Miller	2	Smith	
3	~~Matthews~~	9	(~~Maddox~~) Nichols	3	Herr	●
4	Samuel	5	Ⓐ ~~Scanlon~~ Moore	4	Horner	●
5	~~Diaz~~ 3 Jeltz		Gaipos	5	McGee	
6	~~Carman~~	2	McCall	6	Pena	Ⓢ
7	Jackson	6		7	Lindeman	●
8	Barrett	4		8	Pagnozzi	
9	~~Ruffin~~ Hughes			9	Ort	

EXTRA MEN

LH	RH	LH	RH
~~Horner~~	Erskine, Jordan		
Vukovich	Samuel, Morris		
Cross	Parrish, Kaye		
Daulton	Schu, Cardwell		
Turner	~~Horner~~, Harder		
Jones	Jordan, Nichols		
Jefferson	Gsanto, Levy		

SWITCH HITTERS

Miller

Jeltz

PITCHERS

LH	RH	LH	RH
	Maddux		
	Perrier		
	Moore		
	Tekulve		

Form 63–3/80

108 /   BIG LEAGUE SPRING TRAINING

very little that you can conclude from them, as the chart below indicates. It lists spring-training champions for a ten-year period beginning in 1978. The chart also notes how each team finished in its division during the regular season.

As the chart shows, teams that end up as springtime champions sometimes finish in last place, or close to it, in their division. And the reverse happens too; teams with dismal records in the spring may end up as pennant winners.

Year	Team(s) with Best Spring-Training Record	Regular-Season Division Finish
1978	Detroit Tigers	5
	San Francisco Giants	3
1979	Chicago Cubs	5
1980	Minnesota Twins	3
1981	Detroit Tigers	4
1982	Milwaukee Braves	1
1983	Chicago White Sox	1
1984	San Francisco Giants	6
1985	Toronto Blue Jays	1
1986	Philadelphia Phillies	2
	Pittsburgh Pirates	6
1987	St. Louis Cardinals	1

Some teams play only twenty-five or twenty-six games in the spring. A few teams, however, play as many as thirty games.

Whatever the number, most players feel that they have to play many more games than are necessary and that spring training lasts for too long a time. Boredom begins to develop around the middle of March. Four or five weeks of training would be about right, most players feel.

During the final week the games begin to resemble more closely those of the regular season. Rookies, minor leaguers, and nonroster invitees who have not measured up have been released outright or assigned to the appropriate minor league teams. Hitters have rounded into form. Starting pitchers are pitching six and seven innings with each outing. Relievers are ready, or soon will be.

By the last week of spring training the manager is paying close attention to his pitching selections, for he is striving to get the team's pitching rotation set. The final four or five games before opening day give a pretty fair indication of how a team is going to perform during the season.

By the end of March the manager is ready to announce who will be the team's starting pitcher on opening day. Clubhouse attendants begin packing up the team's equipment and supplies.

Very early in April tractor trailers roll up to the various training camps and everything is loaded into them. Within twenty-four hours the huge trucks are heading north, each bound for a different ballpark.

The players are bused to the local airport. They board the plane that will take them home or to the city where the team is opening the season. They look tanned and rested. The long, demanding season lies ahead.

◆ FURTHER READING

Charlton, Jim, and Shatzkin, Mike. *The Baseball Fan's Guide to Spring Training*. New York: Addison-Wesley Publishing Co., 1988.

Coleman, Ken, with Valenti, Dan. *Grapefruit League Road Trip: A Guide to Spring Training in Florida*. Lexington, Massachusetts: Stephen Greene Press, 1988.

Falkner, David. *The Short Season*. New York: Times Books, 1986.

Honig, Donald. *Up from the Minor Leagues*. New York: Cowles Books, 1970.

◆ INDEX

Page numbers in *italics* indicate illustrations.

113